Poems Hart to Heart

By: Ronald S. Hart

iUniverse, Inc.
New York   Bloomington

iUniverse books may be ordered through booksellers or by contacting:

iUniverse
1663 Liberty Drive
Bloomington, IN 47403
www.iuniverse.com
1-800-Authors (1-800-288-4677)

Because of the dynamic nature of the Internet, any Web addresses or links contained in this book may have changed since publication and may no longer be valid. The views expressed in this work are solely those of the author and do not necessarily reflect the views of the publisher, and the publisher hereby disclaims any responsibility for them.

ISBN: 978-1-4401-6941-0 (sc)
ISBN: 978-1-4401-6942-7 (ebook)

Printed in the United States of America

iUniverse rev. date: 09/15/09

Dedication

Led by the spirit, inspired by the word of God, I would like to dedicate this book of poems to my loving wife of almost 60 years and our family who have supported us both physically and prayerfully in the course of her illness, also to all who have found or are seeking the truth.

The Bible is the authoritative Word of God, we read in 2 Timothy 2: 15, "Study to show thyself approved unto God, a workman that need not be ashamed; 2 Thessalonians 2:15 "Stand fast, and hold the traditions you have been taught." We are saved by Grace through faith, not by our own merit; John 3: 16, "For God so loved the world that He gave his only begotten Son that whosoever believeth on Him shall not perish but have Eternal Life." There is no substitute for the word of God, Hebrews 13:8 "Jesus Christ the same yesterday, today, and forever."

To God Be the Glory.

Ron Hart

Table of Contents

Introduction

Poems Hart to Heart is a collection of seventy – one poems from a man whose deep walk with God is evident in their reading. Anyone reading these poems will find their heart stirred in praise to God, their walk challenged to truly represent godliness in their lives, and their thoughts provoked toward embracing the challenges in their lives.

Mr. Hart grew up on a small farm in the English countryside of East Anglia in what is known there as the Fens. He worked the farm all his working life during which time he continued to grow in his faith and walk with God. Having retired from farming and now in his seventies he dedicates much of his time in devotion to the Lord writing as the Lord lays on his heart. These poems are the product of his walk with God and will surely bless all who read them.

I have the privilege of knowing Mr. Hart as my father-in-law and have spent many hours conversing with him concerning his faith and its application to his life on the farm. In my last visit with him he expressed the desire to have these poems in print. The result of his desire is the product you have before you today. We have purposely left the English spelling of his words in an attempt to truly reflect Mr. Hart.

This book of poems from Mr. Hart, is truly a reflection of *Poems Hart to Heart*.

Dr. and Mrs. Kenneth R. Terry

Ambassadors For Christ

As ambassadors for Christ, how do our lives show?
We are His representatives, to let the world know.
No longer under law, but taught by grace.
And the trials of this world, no longer alone do we face.

No longer a servant, but now a son,
To follow in his footsteps, the work He has done.
The things once impossible we now understand,
The blessing we receive when guided by His hand.

God sent His Son Jesus. It was all in His plan,
That the world might be saved, but not by the works of man.
God so loved the world and in fellowship we will meet,
When walking in the light of our Saviour's feet.

When He finished His creation, God saw that all was well,
Making man in His own image, in the garden to dwell;
Eve, enticed by Satan, caused Adam to sin,
They in the garden, God could no longer allow to live therein.

As we take up our Bibles, we read in its pages,
How man has tested Gods patience, down through the ages.
But in His infinite wisdom, God always knows best,
And in His grace and mercy, man can find complete rest.

God is the good shepherd, calling His sheep back to the fold.
And it's through Jesus, the Way, from His word we are told;
The way back is easy, though narrow and straight,
So start back today, as when Jesus stops calling it will be too late.

Answered Prayer

I prayed a prayer to my God above,
In my quest of what He wanted me to do.
He answered me, "Serve in my love,
That's all I need from you."

By His Spirit in you His love is shown,
If you allow Him His perfect will;
A change in your life as you have never known,
And His love will your heart completely fill.

We find perfect rest in God's garden of peace,
Says God, "Be still and you will find Me;"
When from all unnecessary worldly burdens cease,
May we in faith trust in Thee.

God's word comes to us from above,
Jesus in form of man was sent,
God's Word is shown in brotherly love,
By all who will humbly repent.

God's love is an action towards mankind,
His spirit has taught from His word,
Nothing to match God's love will we ever find.
So reassuring is the voice we have heard.

Assurance

Oh Jesus my Saviour you love me I know.
The stain on your hands the nail prints do show.
Your Grace and your mercy oh so, so divine.
I'm washed by your blood, Salvation is mine.
My Gracious Protector from sin I am saved,
And my pathway to heaven with love it is paved.
Saved by his blood Oh what heavenly bliss,
To know you are bought with a love such as this.

Blessings From God

God gave us eyes to see,
And ears that we might hear.
He gave His spirit to touch our hearts,
And faith that we might not fear.

His guiding hands lead us on the way,
Which He would have us go.
He gave us feet to follow on.
His word teaches all we need to know.

When we allow He leads us on,
Guiding our hands to do His work.
And by His Spirit He gives us voice,
To praise Him in our talk.

We have a lifeline open,
To come to Him in prayer.
His promise to never leave us,
What comfort to know that He is there.

When baptized by His Spirit,
We are no longer in control.
He gives us guidance, peace, and strength.
What comfort to our soul.

God gave his Son to save us,
You may still find this hard to believe.
Open your hearts and ask Him in,
His peace and blessings you will receive.

Can God Use You?

Lord what can I do, as a servant for You,
As I look at others serving as they do.
I feel so inadequate unworthy with fear.
In my helplessness, my prayer, Lord be near.

When I ought to be speaking my tongue keeps still.
To serve others for you Lord I know it's your will.
And fear keeps my mind from what I ought to say.
To bring You praise and glory this I pray.

As I read the Good Book, I see the gifts You give.
Your indwelling Spirit teaches us how to live.
To all who by faith believe in Jesus Your Son,
By Your love the battle over fear has been won.

As we start each day, with a word of prayer.
We thank You Lord in our need You are always there.
By Your guiding Spirit, we absorb Your love,
Guided by a loving hand, reaching down from above.

My prayer now Lord, is show me the need.
And those willing to listen, by Your Word feed.
And those struggling alone weary and depressed,
As we await the day when all will be blessed.

No longer a servant, accepted as a son.
The victory over death and Satan Jesus has won.
Your love for us has conquered our fear.
We give thanks and praise for your presence so near.

Not by works but saved by grace.

No longer the trials of this world alone do we face.

Keeping us humble and trusting our hope from above,

When safe in the fold of Your bountiful love.

Christ's Morning

Christmas, the morning of Jesus our Lord's day of birth.

Bringing glad tidings to all the nations of the earth.

Born of the virgin Mary, He came as a small child,

Not as a tyrant king, a baby meek and mild.

Born in a lowly manger, no room at the inn,

Not in a warm bed, just the heat from the animals within.

The shepherds on the hillside, and in the sky a bright star,

Guiding the wise men, bringing their gifts, from a country afar.

The news of this birth, filled Herod's heart with fear,

He tried hard to find Him, to kill Him it was clear.

God sent an angel, to warn the wise men, not let Herod know,

And to foil him, to take another way home, as they go.

In a dream to warn Joseph, an angel God sent,

And instead of going to his home, to Egypt he went.

When Herod heard this, he was so angry, and self willed,

Ordered all the children under two years old to be killed.

Then was fulfilled, what Jeremiah's prophecy meant,

In Rama mothers weeping, and was heard a lament.

An angel again in a dream, told Joseph Herod was dead,

"Take the young child and his mother into Egypt," the angel said.

When Joseph heard, in Judea was Herod's son, he was afraid,

Being warned of God, towards Galilee, the journey he made.

To dwell in the city called Nazareth, he came,

Fulfilling that spoken by the prophets, called a Nazarene by name.

John the Baptist came preaching in the wilderness, saying repent,
For the kingdom of heaven is at hand, the Messiah has been sent.
To gather his wheat in his garner, and the chaff to burn,
Baptizing with the Holy Spirit, to all who to Him will turn.

John Baptized with water, and in the river Jordan they went,
When Jesus came to him for baptism, at first John wouldn't consent.
"To fulfill all righteousness," Jesus said "This must be done,"
And lo a voice from heaven, saying, "This is my beloved Son."

God had a plan, for his Son Jesus this He did send,
Who gave His life a ransom, to be the sinner's friend.
God so loves the world, and by his mercy and His grace,
Calling all who through faith in Jesus, to His heavenly place.

Citizens of God's Household.

No more strangers, but citizens of God's household,
In Christ's name, His elect, and safe within His fold.
In His Father's will, He took our place, it was our debt no more,
He gave His life, and paid the price, His promise ever sure.

When He returned to His Father's side, His spirit He did send,
To dwell within to guide us, and on whom we can depend.
We are Gods temple, a place where He can abide,
And by His grace, we are saved, while we keep close beside.

The Holy Spirit speaks to us, when we read God's word,
There is no voice like His that we have ever heard.
It reaches down into our hearts, so quiet and yet so strong,
Bringing us peace and joy, and in our hearts a song.

Between the spirit and the flesh, there is no middle ground,
And when the seal is finally broken, we trust our name is found.
There will be no room for excuse, for the word of God is sure,
And all who believe in His Son will live with Him evermore.

It was not our choice, we are chosen in Christ's precious name,
We never could afford the debt we owe, this is why Jesus came.
For God so loved the world, and by His mercy and His grace,
And by our faith, at judgment day, Jesus will stand in our place.

When worldly troubles surround us, may we never fear,
As His promise to be always with us, and His presence ever near.
His love is unconditional, with the blessings that He sends,
And the rewards, He has for us, when this world finally ends.

When Jesus comes again, it will be with great power,
And may we be ever watchful, for we know not the hour.
God's word is sure, and it is plainly there for us to know,
That if Jesus came tonight, would we all be ready to go.

Exhortation Towards Life

God has given us a mind, that we might keep learning,
All scripture is inspired, and is profitable, may we keep yearning.
Instructed in righteousness, to perfect us, we have Christ's mind,
We are God's temple, His pleasure, and His presence we find.

God's love keeps us loving, it's His will that to others we show,
Bearing each other's burdens, that they may also of His love know.
God sent His Son, Jesus, a living sacrifice, who died to set us free,
From the burden of sin, turning darkness to light, that we might see.

May our hearts be filled with laughter, as together we share,
The joyful blessings God sends us, casting on Him all our care.
By confession God forgives us, we can leave all our sins behind,
Moving on towards our heavenly goal, where His glory we will find.

In our dreams we feel longing, guiding us through life in Jesus' way,
Putting aside worldly wisdom, to lean on Jesus more everyday.
To lean on Jesus is to trust Him, and we find His promise ever sure,
Bringing our trials to Him, He hears us, let's Praise Him evermore.

Looking to God for guidance, and strength, a focus for our walk,
The Holy Spirit, our teacher, to comfort and control us in our talk.
He will bring to our remembrance, all Jesus ever did or said,
May we walk worthy of our vocation, for Christ He is our Head.

As we labour on together, with our faith strong and sure,
Clothed in His righteousness, bringing glory to Him evermore.
By our mouth may we confess, a loving Saviour to behold,
As we read from our Bibles the greatest story ever told.

May our speech be with understanding, that the lost may hear,
For God would have none perish, His perfect love casts out all fear.
May we be a willing listener, as the Spirit prompts us from the word,
And the voice that bids us welcome, is the sweetest ever heard.

Faith and Hope

As the dawn brings forth the sunrise,
To herald in each new day,
I find it is the best time,
To read God's word and pray.

What better way to start the day,
Than to spend time with God in prayer;
To read His word, and meditate and pray,
For we find our prayers answered there.

God so loved His creation He formed,
He sent forth his only begotten Son.
To save the world and restore again,
What Satan had undone.

In the garden of Eden, Adam's rebellious act,
Condemned the world to sin.
But the blood of Christ opened heaven's door again,
That all who believe this could enter in.

It is by faith in a loving Saviour,
By the mystery of faith we are set free.
Faith is our hope and hope that's not seen,
If we could see faith would no longer be.

When Jesus returned to his Father's side,
His promise, the Father the Comforter would send;
And for us is preparing mansions to be,
For our calling home is the beginning - not the end.

We patiently await our Saviour's return,
As He promised we read in His word;
To separate the sheep from the goats,
Our hope is to be in that heavenly herd.

Faith not Feeling

We are not saved by feelings, but by fact.
It is God's love for us, not by how we act;
God said, "I am Alpha and Omega, the beginning and the end,"
He knew man's rebellious ways, for this reason His Son did send.

Not by works, could we God's righteousness attain.
Christ bore our sin upon the cross and then He arose again.
No longer are we under the law, but in God's saving grace,
No matter what the consequence, no more alone do we face.

Gods purpose from the beginning, to provide His Son a bride.
The bride, the church, built by faith, which no one can divide.
We know not when, but He is coming back, this marriage will take place.
What a glorious day, when in heaven, we will meet Him face to face.

This is the promise He has given us, written in His word.
He has chosen us, may we accept, His voice is the sweetest ever heard.
As we journey through this life, we find nothing can compare,
To the love we find in Jesus, and His blessings that we share.

In times of trial, we need not despair, turn to the Lord and pray.
And if we feel He has not heard, it's not rejection but delay.
He patiently awaits our requests, for our needs to receive.
Humbly casting our care on Him, and our burdens He will relieve.

As ambassadors for Christ, His church together we stand,
Upholding each other in faith, guided by His hand;
The fields are white to harvest, and the reapers they are few.
Revival like charity starts at home, let's begin with me and you.

Those that have not heard of Jesus, and those who have rejected His call,
God, He so loved the world, and the gospel message is for all.
He sent His only begotten Son, as a living sacrifice for our sin,
But only those with believing faith, will in heaven be allowed in.

God's Armour

No where are we promised an easy road,
But we are promised, help with the burden of our load.
As soldiers of Christ, are we ready to go,
To the world's battlefields, and face the foe?

Be strong in the Lord, and in the power of His might,
Putting on Gods armour, for it's the wiles of the devil we fight.
We wrestle not against flesh and blood, but the sinking sand,
Of the powers and the rulers of darkness, we have to stand.

May the armour of righteousness, be our breastplate,
Our loins girded by the truth, that we might relate.
To the gospel of peace, may our feet we prepare,
To a lost world, show through us Jesus does care.

The shield of faith, may we hold in our hand,
Quenching the fiery darts of the wicked, which we have to withstand.
Taking the helmet of salvation, as we await our reward,
Trusting God's word, which for the Spirit is a sword.

May our supplication in the Spirit be our prayer,
Claiming Jesus' promise, He would always be there.
Not provoking to others, but teaching in love,
Pleasing to the Father, as He looks down from above.

Be kind to one another, tender hearted, forgiveness revealed,
Grieving not the Spirit, whereby unto the day of redemption we are sealed.
Sometimes we were in darkness, now in the light of the Lord we find,
By putting on the new man, the renewing of the mind,

Jesus the propitiation for our sins, no other foundation can be laid,
For we His workmanship, set apart for good works, the price been paid.
Justified by faith are all who on Jesus believe,
But the wrath of God abides, on all who will not Jesus receive

God Knows Best

God does not always move the mountain, or part the rolling sea,
With trials He tests us, teaching us patience, whatever the trial may be.
He is standing on the front line, watching every move and step we take,
And if we fall, we feel His guiding hand, He promised never to forsake.

We don't hear much spoken of the devil today, as if He is gone for good,
But the word of God does not teach this, for if it was so it would.
The enemy is so subtle, in temptation, and encouraging towards sin he can be,
The word of God says, draw close to me, resist the devil and he will flee,

The harvest fields are ready, with souls waiting to be gathered in,
The reapers are few, will all the souls be gathered, and saved from sin?
For God said, whosoever believes in Jesus His only begotten Son,
Would never perish, He has paid the price, and the work is done.

If we walk in the light as Jesus is light, with fellowship we share,
Cleansed by His Blood, safe in His arms, and in His loving care.
When He left to be with the Father, He prayed His Spirit He would send,
Now we have the indwelling Spirit, guiding us until our journeys end.

Sitting at his Father's right hand, in Heaven where our hope is one day to be,
He is waiting the day to come again, but the time is not for us to see.
When He is coming to gather his church, as His bride on her wedding day,
As His ambassadors there is work to be done, but for His coming we pray.

God's Garden

The world is God's garden,
And sin is the weeds.
The church is His flowers,
Grown from His own seed.

The devil has sown,
The tares in the wheat;
The church is God's workers,
To build His retreat.

God nurtures His flowers,
With his unfailing love;
It falls like the showers,
And sends from above.

When watered by love,
The church it does grow;
The fields white to harvest,
And ready to mow.

The harvest is ready,
The reapers are few;
The spirit is willing,
To bring life anew.

The church on its own,
Cannot convict of sin;
It's the spirit that convicts,
And works from within.

The body of man,
Is the temple of God;
Who dares defile the temple,
Where God's spirit has trod?

God's Let Us Salad.

Let us fear, lest the entering of His rest, we don't receive,
We have heard the Gospel, as did those who did not believe.
They would not accept, God's only begotten Son whom He sent,
Carrying on as before, taking no heed, and would never repent.

Let us labour therefore, that we might gain entrance into his rest,
By our faith in Jesus, not as the unbelieving and failing His test.
For God's word is the truth, sharper than a two-edged sword,
Quick, and powerful, to all who knowingly disobey His word.

Let us come boldly, therefore not by merit, to His throne of grace,
That we might obtain mercy, and not have alone the judgement to face.
God knows all His children, and who in Jesus their fruits do show,
Not all who say "Lord" will enter His rest, only He has right to say no.

Let us go on, He has paved the way, now may we do the walk,
For believing faith without works is dead, it is not just talk.
When we commit our lives to Jesus, it's a beginning not an end,
Then as we journey on together, on Him can we fully depend.

Let us draw near, to Him who dispels all our anxieties and fear,
Showing love to all others, as He has watched over and loved us so dear.
Through trials and temptation, if we are troubled and feel the need,
He is never more than a prayer away, as when on His word we feed.

Let us hold fast, and our faith keep steady and strong,
Resisting the evil one, trusting the Lord to keep us from wrong.
God's word and his Spirit, never contradict, always the same,
Jesus redeemed us from lost eternity, for this reason He came.

Let us consider and pray for one another, for this is God's will,

If we walk in the light, as Jesus is light, in fellowship we fulfill.

No longer servants, but sons and heirs, exhorting each other in love,

As His ambassadors, pleasing our Lord, as he looks down from above

God's Reapers

God's harvest of souls is for Thanksgiving,
The fruit of His labour from above;
We share in the light of His glory,
Produced in heaven by His love.

He has called His saints for His reapers
To store in His garner evermore;
To bring the lost home to His kingdom,
Where in safety forever He will store.

We the saints are called to be sowers,
In His furrow to sow seeds of love;
In His grace we are to cultivate kindness,
As His mercy He showers from above.

We are powered by the blessed Holy spirit,
The lights in His kingdom below;
When our blessed Lord returns in His glory,
The gift of salvation on us He will bestow.

There is a warning to all who reject him,
Who for this old world have craved.
For we the saints were once lost sinners,
But now we are sinners but saved.

God has called all in his grace and mercy,
The message of the gospel revealed.
Although the wound of our sin is still open,
Jesus Christ by His blood He has healed.

God's Purpose

God has a purpose that comes with His plan,
The reason He sent His Holy Spirit to dwell in man.
He was sent as a teacher, a comforter, and guide,
As the fruits of the Spirit are taught from the inside.

Love like a reflection, comes from God first,
Reflected towards us, for his love may we thirst.
In sorrows and trials, the joy that it brings.
With praise and thanksgiving our hearts sing.

We each have a cross, we have been given to bear,
Which is made easier, when in fellowship we share.
Although the cross may seem heavy, it's never above,
Our weakest endurance, and covered by His love.

He teaches contentment, in humbleness we bow,
With peace and longsuffering, seeds of kindness we sow.
We are taught how to forgive, by His everlasting love,
By His in-dwelling Spirit, sent down from above.

On that great and final day, when Jesus comes in power,
We will meet those gone before, who await this glorious hour.
There is a place prepared in heaven for who in faith believe,
To be at home with Jesus, what a blessing to receive.

So my friend if Jesus beckons, respond to His call,
Put your trust in Him and give him your all.
There is a day coming, which no one knows the date,
Or like the five virgins with no oil, it will be too late.

God's Temple.

Know ye not that our bodies are Gods temple,
Wherein dwells the Holy Spirit, our Father God did send.
He came at Jesus request, as a guide, to strengthen, and comfort,
We are never alone, and he will be with us until the end.

To be born again, is to be born of the Holy Spirit,
Confirmed by Gods word, which never changes always the same.
No one can say Jesus is Lord, but by the Holy Spirit,
A lamp to our feet, this is why Jesus He came.

Who can separate us from God's love, when saved by His grace,
Sanctified by Jesus' blood, no longer in bondage by the law.
Heirs of God through Christ, no more servants but sons,
Finding peace and reconciliation, we had never tasted before.

Born of the Spirit, by the Spirit may we walk,
Not be weary in well doing, then in due season we will reap.
Called unto liberty, but not to use as an occasion to the flesh,
Bearing one another's burdens, the Lord's command to keep.

If in this world only, in Christ we have hope,
And if Christ be not risen, is our preaching but vain.
For we are saved by hope, but hope that is not seen,
Our hope builds our faith, as with Jesus we reign.

Hopeless we may feel, but by Gods grace we are what we are,
Thanks be to God, we have the victory in Jesus Christ our Lord.
Not that we loved God, but that God loved us,
Paid in full, the debt we owe, which to pay we could not afford.

Although the time unknown, the day is getting closer,
When Jesus will come, in a cloud, with power and great glory.
May we be ready, as we patiently await, and in him abiding,
His promise to us Eternal life, and the promise is his story.

God's Way Prevails

Hated by his brothers, but was his father's joy,
Rachel was his mother, and Jacob His father's favourite boy.
God gave him the gift of prophecy, Joseph was his name,
He had a dream, which caused his families hearts to inflame.

He saw one day they would all bow to him, and told them so,
They were not impressed, and anyway how could he know?
His father spoke harshly to him, his mother kept them in mind,
His brothers kept his father's flocks, and sent Joseph for them to find.

His father made him a coat of many colours, he stood out in a crowd,
The brothers saw him coming, "Here comes that dreamer," they cried aloud.
They sought out to kill him, but Reuben thought it not fit,
He said, "Let's not kill him, but throw him in that pit."

Later when Reuben returned to the pit, only to be told,
A caravan of Midianites passed by, and to them Joseph they sold.
Who sold him on to Potiphar, who found him honest and true,
He was put in charge of the Royal household, and all there was to do.

Potiphar's wife became fond of him, tried to seduce him one day,
But leaving his scarf behind, escaped the house and ran away.
When Potiphar returned was angry, and Joseph to jail was sent,
But soon found favour, for God was with him everywhere he went.

In jail the Butler and Baker both had dreams, and were afraid,
Joseph said his God would interpret, and on his knees he prayed.
God told Joseph, the butler would be restored, the baker killed,
Then Pharaoh had a dream, and with fear his heart was filled.

Joseph prayed God would Pharaoh's dream explain,
It was of the good years and the bad years, of the famine to maintain.
Joseph was made responsible in the good years, the wheat to store,
Through Joseph God had made provision, there would be food as before.

Jacob sent his sons to buy, when in Egypt he heard there was wheat,
For the famine was hitting hard, and they had very little to eat.
When the brothers heard who Joseph was, it filled their heart with fright,
"Don't blame yourselves," Joseph said, "God who sent me to make things right."

Gone But Not Forgotten

The cross has long been gone, upon which our Saviour died,
The cruel pains and agony He must have felt, rejected and alone.
Pierced by the sword, the blood and water gushed from his side,
His sacrifice at His Father's will, it was for us to atone.

The stone that sealed the tomb, they found rolled away,
The tomb was empty, only the grave cloths folded neat.
No earthly power could hold him, His promise on the third day,
To build His temple in three days, bringing us to the mercy seat.

He told His disciples He had to go, His promise to come again,
And He would pray the Father, the Comforter He would send.
Bringing Him to our remembrance, preparing us with Him to reign,
Saying He would never leave or forsake us, to be with us unto the end.

The comforter works within us, like the potter with his clay,
He encourages us, curbs our thoughts, until like Christ's is our mind.
Helps us understand God's word, at the thought of sin we feel dismay,
He lovingly chastens us, to walk His way, and the pleasure we find.

Saved by grace, through faith, salvation to us is free,
Set apart for service, to further the Gospel is our task.
To walk in Jesus footsteps, his ambassadors, that all might see,
That in all our trials he helps us, all we have to do is ask.

May we use the gift given us, and let not His Spirit grieve,
Exhorting one another, shedding light for the blind to see.
To share another's burden with them, the blessings we receive,
We see the Father's love in Jesus, from sin setting us free.

God so loved the world, He gave His only Son,
That whosoever believed in Him, eternal life would give.
The battle with the evil one, now forever has been won,
And one day we will all meet in heaven, with our Lord to live.

Have You Met With Jesus?

If you have never met with Jesus, meet with Him today,
No appointment to make, no forms to fill, all we need to do is pray.
The words we use will profit us, the best we will ever make,
And receive the promise of Eternal Life, even for His Father's name sake.

He makes no judgment, no trial for sin we have to face,
Just acknowledge we are sinners, He pardons us by grace.
From this moment onwards, He sends his Spirit within us to dwell,
No more to face the world alone, the way forward for us He will tell.

The past is gone, no way could we go back to put things right,
Only God by His Son Jesus, could die to make us Holy in His sight.
Jesus is the way to Eternal Life, no other way can we find,
When God sent His Son to earth, it was the sinner he had in mind.

Jesus knows our faults, yet in us He only believes the best,
We humbly put our faith in Him, trusting His Spirit to do the rest.
Jesus is the same today, tomorrow, forever, for our good He has a plan,
He has a place prepared in heaven for us, the time unknown to man.

The sinner in the world, with a Holy God is out of reach,
Jesus is the sinner's friend, His spirit from the word does teach.
All have sinned and short of God's glory, the wages of sin is death,
Today is the day of salvation, turn to Jesus while we still have breath.

We have a birthright it's Jesus, from the Bible we are told,
Not to be like Esau, who for a bowl of soup, his birthright sold.
With no oil the five virgins, when the bridegroom came they could not see,
It's not God's will that any should perish, to a lost eternity.

To the sinner without Jesus a lifeline is thrown,
Like a lamb to the slaughter, His death for us he did atone.
Reconciling us back to the Father, who cannot look upon sin,
Has opened up the road to Eternal Life, that we might enter in.

He Has Never Left Us

My friend have you never heard,
Believe it for its true;
How Jesus left His Fathers throne,
To die for me and you.

He came to earth a lowly child,
His mother watched Him grow;
His whole life He spent at His Father's command,
An example for us to go.

Our Father God so much He loved,
This world so full of sin;
That he gave His only Son to unlock the gate,
Of heaven and let us in.

There is only one way through that heavenly gate,
And Jesus Christ He holds the key;
The price He paid on that cruel cross,
And He did it for you and me.

They laid His body in a tomb,
And watched it all night long;
And in the morn His friends they came,
And found that it had gone.

Once more He showed Himself again,
To His friends all filled with gloom;
At the supper He said His last farewell
To his friends in that upper room.

He promised He would never leave us alone,
As back to his Fathers throne He went;
And Jesus, Saviour, and Lord, is true to his word,
For his Father His Spirit he sent.

Hope Not Seen

As believers we live in hope, through faith and not seen,
Trusting God's word is our hope, and on Jesus we earnestly lean.
Our hope is in His grace, bringing salvation to all and free,
In the cross is our hope, where Jesus died for you and me.

Not by our works could we reach, His holy standards set,
We do not deserve His promise, our sins, to forgive and forget.
Sanctified, by Jesus Blood, from the world have been set free,
Clothed by His righteousness, once was blind but now we can see.

He is our shepherd, like sheep following in His footsteps day by day,
In our need, we look to Him, to guide us along the way.
Sometimes when the road seems impossible, it's good to know He is there,
He is willingly awaiting our call, when we go to Him in prayer.

He has set us apart, to enjoy Fellowship with Him so sweet,
The longing in our hearts to be fulfilled, when face to face we meet.
This world is but a wilderness, on our journey to the promised land,
And the manna we receive each day, given by His loving hand.

One day we know not when, and the judgment seat we face,
Cleansed from our sin, by Jesus Blood, now He will take our place;
There is no condemnation, to whom Jesus is Saviour and Lord,
Sacrificing Himself, paying the price, a debt we could not afford.

My friends if this world is your home, and Jesus is not your choice,
Tarry awhile, listen for His call, and hearken to His voice;
He does not demand or force, He welcomes all in love,
Then in faith is our hope, that one day in heaven we will meet in His home above.

How Precious the Blood

That precious blood which on Calvary Hill was shed,
Once flowed through our loving Saviour's veins.
Like a lamb to the slaughter He was led,
He did it for us, at his Father's will, with love unfeigned.

A once for all sacrifice He did make,
As an appeasement, as no one else had the power.
The cup of suffering, to drink He did take,
He did it for us, that the Father on us His blessing shower.

He had thousands of angels He could call at hand,
Who could have lifted Him down from that cross.
But the cords of love that held Him, He made His stand,
He did it for us, for without it would have been our loss.

God so loved the sinner, but hated the sin,
That he sent His only begotten Son, on that cross to die.
Pardoned by grace, in Jesus, redemption we did win,
He did it for us, that we might all meet together By and By.

One day we all before the judgment seat will appear,
For the things we have done, whether good or bad.
With our names written in the book life, we have no fear,
He did it for us, but for the unredeemed how sad.

To love others from the word we have been taught,
By this our discipleship, by all men will be known.
By the word and the Spirit, by Jesus' example to live and exhort,
He did it for us, the seeds of loving kindness He has sown.

He has gone on before us, preparing in His mansions a room,
That one day we will join Him, when He welcomes us home.
What a blessing for us, when they looked, finding empty the tomb,
He did it for us, safe in his arms, no longer to roam.

In God's Time

We know not when, the day, the hour,
Only God knows for He has the power.
We only can be prepared, it is our choice,
To walk with Jesus, and listening for His voice.

In His own time, we wait, in hope, to hear His call,
We need not fear, while in His care, whatever may befall.
His guiding Spirit, will lead us each step of the way,
If we accept Jesus Christ as Saviour, and His will we obey.

Born of Adam's race, in the flesh, of guilt and sin,
In this world alone, without hope, without His Holy Spirit within.
Not saved by our merit, but by God's love, mercy, and grace,
And to satisfy our heavenly Father, Jesus stands in our place.

This world is but a wilderness, as we journey to the promised land,
When we cross over the river Jordan, and on the other shore to stand.
Though the Sun and Moon be darkened, we will not need their light,
We will see our blessed Saviour, and His glory shining bright.

Satan no more to taunt us, cast in the bottomless pit,
We will see the heavenly throne, where our Saviour He will sit.
When the final seal is broken, and is opened up the book,
May our names be found written, for the judgment He will look.

No more tears, no more sorrow, our hope eternal joy,
And the loved ones gone before us, once more their company to enjoy.
With the heavenly host keep praising, Jesus as our Lord,
He took our place, our redeemer, the one to be adored.

Clothed in His righteousness, made holy, set apart to serve,
A mansion in His Father's house, His promise to reserve.
For His work He gave us gifts, to heal the sick by prayer,
His purpose for us, to a lost world, our testimony to share.

In Jesus' Name

When we are born again, we take on our Saviour's name,
We are to put on the new man, never again to be the same.
Indwelt by the Holy Spirit, His purpose as Comforter and Guide,
Sent by the Father, at Jesus request, may we by Him abide.

If we allow him, He reminds us what we have read in God's word,
The law was our schoolmaster, leading us to the greatest story ever heard.
It's about a baby born to the virgin Mary, Gods only begotten Son,
Then he returned to his Father's side when His work on earth was done.

His purpose to bring reconciliation, of man back to God in main,
For since the fall of man, in no way could man his own salvation gain;
Only His Son Jesus, could pay the full debt owed by man for sin,
And it is by grace not merit, we have the kingdom of God within.

Jesus taught, blessed are the poor in spirit, and also the meek,
The pure in heart, and all who after righteousness do seek;
The merciful, the peacemakers, those persecuted for His sake,
For great the rewards in heaven, Rejoice, for the blessings they make.

There is no law, when the fruits of the Spirit we do show,
We have no excuse, for the Spirit and the Word teach us so.
God is love, which covers all, and in love we ought to live,
And when we feel the hurt of others, He teaches us how to forgive.

When we do not forgive, all the love from our hearts it will drain,
And when we forgive, we pass it to God, and let Him take the strain.
His Spirit does lead us, and by the fruits of his Spirit may we walk,
For love is an action, which goes out to others, and not only just talk.

God never changes, His word is truth, of justice and love,
And our faith will be rewarded, when He calls us to His home above;
Jesus came to save, not condemn, to force or reject,
God loves all, but without faith, salvation will have no effect.

I Wondered Why?

I wondered why I felt today,
No one would really care,
But we never really know,
How many have thought of us in prayer.

I wondered why I felt this way
So much so I was in despair,
Then I heard the voice of Jesus say,
"Do come to me in prayer."

I wondered why I felt this way
For God placed His hand in mine;
He said, "Don't think so much of you, but pray
And trust and don't decline."

No longer did I feel this way
My faith grew stronger and sure;
As I read in His word His promise I heard,
In His Glory I will share evermore.

Jesus our Assurance

When we walk in the light, as Jesus is light,
Following in His footsteps, by faith and not sight.
In humble submission, we can defeat the prince of the air,
Jesus is a lamp unto our feet, if we trust in his care.

Jesus has completed His work, for His Father here on earth,
Bringing salvation to all who believe, giving us a new birth.
The devil will do his utmost, to distract us by laying a snare,
But he is no match for Jesus, we have no need to despair.

The devils favourite pastime, is setting brother against brother,
Sowing discord, instead of harmony and love for one another.
The word gives us the answer, if to the Holy Spirit we give heed,
For His fruits give us the power, to resist and it's all we ever need.

The devil still roams to and fro, although not all would agree,
The Bible teaches he does, but if we submit to God he will flee.
Although he has lost his power, he will never give in,
His greatest ambition is to keep the world in sin.

The devils greatest victory is when we deny he exists,
Even the word tells us, submit to God and to the devil resist.
We wrestle not against flesh and blood, but principalities and power,
May we put on Gods armour, for protection in our darkest hour.

Created in Christ Jesus unto good works, therefore we stand,
With the breastplate of righteousness, the shield of faith in hand.
The helmet of salvation, and His word we hold as our sword,
As the messengers of the gospel, with the truth from His word.

Gods love will never falter, to whom in Him put their trust,
The blessings we receive by grace, no more for the world we lust;
The devil may try to entice us, but never may we fear,
For Jesus is Lord and Saviour, to Him we are so dear.

Jesus Redeemer and Judge

Are you burdened down and no one seems to care?
We have a friend in Jesus, take it to Him in prayer.
Whatever the burden, He is always ready and willing to hear,
Trust Him, He will lighten the burden, and cast away the fear.

He is a willing listener, whether it's to praise or a request,
Give Him the praise and glory, for us He only wants the best.
His name above all names, for our sin an advocate,
Accept Him, salvation is for today, tomorrow maybe too late.

His word teaches us, in each circumstance we have to face,
He soothes our every sorrow, when covered by his grace.
For anger and bitterness, only eats into our soul,
When we forgive each other, in love we are made whole.

In obedience to His Father's will, in humiliation and pain,
We may not understand this fully, until he comes again.
He did it for our salvation, unto good works we are ordained,
Created in Christ Jesus, His workmanship, to live our life unfeigned.

Salvation is a new beginning, to begin our lives anew,
Each one of us has differing gifts, for there are many works to do.
Some may do more, and some may do less, but it not just the amount,
It's not what we do, but how it's done, we will have to give an account.

For what we have done good or bad, just will be our reward,
Saved by His grace, we are not condemned, if Jesus is our Lord.
No matter what we do or say, we know not when, but He will call,
His faithful will not perish, for the gospel message is for all.

There will be a final judgment, when God's wrath is shown,
No second chance, for those whose names are not known.
Jesus stands knocking, at the door of your heart, will you let Him in,
On the cross He paid the price, to save the world, a sacrifice for sin.

John's Vision

John in his vision saw coming down a new heaven and earth,
The old heaven and earth passing away, to herald in its birth.
This is the promise Jesus made to his friends, before leaving that day,
That one day he is coming back, forever with His loved ones to stay.

The sun and moon will be darkened, no longer needed to give light,
For the glory of Jesus, Gods only begotten Son, will be shining so bright.
It has been revealed when He comes, He is coming to judge towards sin,
The door will be closed, and none but by the Blood of Jesus will enter therein.

By faith we accept this vision, for we believe Gods word is true,
And that Jesus has prepared a place with His loved ones in view.
There is a place reserved for us, it is ours to make the choice,
He will not always call, may we accept Him when we hear His voice.

When this world ends, no longer will the wheat and tares together grow,
The meaning of this parable, as the tares are gathered we already know.
The good seed are the children of the kingdom, the tares of the wicked one,
There will be wailing and gnashing of teeth, when this work has to be done.

As we read our Bibles, and meditating our thoughts taking God at His word,
It's His truth not to be took lightly, how receptive are we to what we have heard.
God's word is a complete volume, if He has only half He has none,
If we add to it or take away, and if Satan has half he has already won.

Journey of life

This life is but a journey, we are traveling heavenward we believe,
God gave us this promise in His word, to all who would receive.
In heaven there are many mansions, Jesus is preparing for us one day,
And by faith our hope to be in the number, who will be going there to stay.

There is only one road we can travel, to reach this heavenly place,
And as we travel homeward, there will be many obstacles to face.
God has not promised us an easy road, free from trials to bear,
And by faith our hope is in Jesus, who in our trials He will share

This journey is not for us to boast, we are traveling in God's plan,
God sent His Son called Jesus, for it is not by the works of man.
When on the cross He paid the debt for sin, for us then and there,
And by faith our hope is in Jesus, for we know he does really care.

As we travel on this journey, in joy we face its trials and woe,
For in the trials God plans for us, we find strength and patience we know.
Jesus promised He would never leave us, asked the Father His Spirit to send,
By faith our hope is in Jesus, who in heaven will meet at the journey's end.

So father, mother, sister, brother, if you feel this journey you would like to take,
For besides grace and mercy, He is a God of justice, a decision you must make.
There is only one road to heaven, through Jesus God's only begotten Son,
And by faith our hope is in Jesus, for the battle over evil He has won.

So if you decide to make this journey, you never will regret,
For Jesus is The Way, The Truth, The life, in whom the Father has beset.
And on the cross at Calvary, His shed Blood, for sin paid in full the debt,
And by faith our hope is in Jesus, for it was for our sin, His death He met.

As we travel on this journey, there are many friends to whom we meet,
Who like us have been forgiven, finding hope at the mercy seat;
Jesus did not come to condemn the world, but through Him might be saved,
And by faith our hope is in Jesus, who by grace the way He has paved.

Just for Us

Those outstretched arms,
The pieced hands and feet,
Call welcome all to me,
Come to the mercy seat.

The cords of love that held him there,
Stronger than any rope.
He took the shame of all our sin,
Creating in us our hope.

He willingly endured the pain,
The suffering and humility.
He did it all without thought of gain
In love for you and me.

He could have called an army of angels,
To lift Him down from the cross.
But that was not his Fathers will,
And that would have been our loss.

He knew the burden of sin and shame,
The pieced hands and feet,
Call welcome all to me
Come to the mercy seat.

The nailed pieced hands,
The sword gashed side,
The blood and water flowed,
It was for us he died.

A guard was placed outside the tomb,
But the battle had been won.
Next morning the stone was rolled away,
And his body it was gone.

His work on earth had now been done,
The debt been paid in full.
Not by merit of our own, but by His grace,
Which no one can annul.

To the one who gave so much,
What can we give or bring.
But to the glory of His name,
And to His praise we sing.

Knowing He Is There

At the start of each new day,
As we bow our heads in prayer.
We thank God for the privilege
Of knowing He is there.

God is a willing listener,
As to Him our troubles we pour.
If He does not always answer,
It does not mean He loves us no more.

God never forgets His church,
Although we wander far astray.
His arms are forever welcoming us,
Back to Him when we pray.

We know we are not worthy,
But by His grace and love.
Jesus our Lord and Redeemer,
Was sent from heaven above.

God so loved the world,
Although it was dark with sin.
Jesus for our sins He died,
And cleansed us from within.

What can we bring our Saviour,
Who fulfils our every need.
We can only show our love for Him,
As to the lost His word we feed.

Learning God's Ways

Before we can run, we have to learn how to walk,
Before we can speak, we have to learn how to talk.
We can't run from God, as there's nowhere to hide,
God will not hear us speak, unless we with him abide.

Jonah, God's command he attempted to ignore,
Almost lost his life, then whale threw him out on the shore.
God's word is His bond, which we must obey,
And endure His chastening, for this is His way.

Before we can walk with God, we must know His will,
We find this in His word, which the Holy Spirit doth instill.
Our faith comes by hearing, and hearing by God's word,
As He calls us to His kingdom, the sweetest voice ever heard.

We walk trusting Jesus, for our faith and hope is not seen,
We walk in His footsteps, to places we have never been.
Together we are His body, and He is the head,
Each has his task, feeding His sheep, until all have been fed.

He is the Great Shepherd, who watches over His own,
To our Father in heaven, through his Son Jesus we are known.
Whatever may befall us, we have no need to fear,
For Jesus has promised, He will always be near.

As each day passes by, we the seeds of hope to the lost sow,
And by our love and kindness, may it be nurtured and grow.
The world is watching us, so by our example may we be,
Reapers for the harvest, to set the lost sinners free.

It is by our actions, we fulfill Gods purpose for His plan,
To live our lives as Jesus did when He was here as a man.
His Spirit He sent to guide us, to help us his ways to understand,
We will never be lonely or discouraged, while guided by His loving hand

Leaning on Faith

Faith is God's gift to us, and it's by faith and not sight we walk.
Helping us to follow in His footsteps, and guide us in our talk.
He is well pleased, when His kingdom and righteousness we seek,
And He rains down showers of blessings on the humble and the meek.

In His Loving kindness, He comforts those who in sorrow mourn,
And we feel our load grow lighter, as our burdens He has borne.
Blessed are the merciful, as are the pure in heart,
And the rewards He has for us, in heaven He will one day impart.

In trials and persecutions, He watches, and is never far away,
At times like this if we feel the need, He is waiting for us to pray.
Blessed are the peacemakers, in humbleness to others do show,
God's love to us, and others through us might come to know.

God gave us His word, and His Spirit, so with others we might share,
His longsuffering loving kindness, showing He really does care.
He gives us more than we deserve, not by merit but by grace,
Not by our works, or in His judgment we would have to face.

Faith gives us sight, into our hope and in our final rest,
God allows at times trials for us to endure, putting us to test.
But never more temptation, than we can escape or bear.
He loves us so, that when we ask in faith He answers our prayer.

If the salt has lost its savour, what more good can it be,
And a light hid under a bushel, gives no light for us to see.
May we use the gift He has given us, whether voice or hand,
Then when Satan tempts us, submit to God, and make our stand.

Life's Challenge

Life is a challenge, from the cradle to the grave,
From the first breath we take, we are taught how to behave.
To sit up, then crawl, and then to stand and walk,
And then to make funny noises, until we can talk.

At this point we do not realize our life is in God's hand.
The mystery of the Gospel is too much for us to understand.
We have a God given conscience, to teach us right from wrong,
For this is our challenge that stays with us all our life long.

The challenge of the world, so easy for us to forget,
For they are manmade, and by man have been set.
But the greatest challenge, we will ever face,
Is the challenge of Jesus, when saved by His grace.

As we travel life's road we find many challenges to face,
And many would be impossible, but for God's grace.
For Satan is the enemy of God, so spiritual warfare we find,
Although he has been defeated, he can still undermine.

Our challenges are not against flesh and blood, but principalities and powers,
We need to stand steadfast in our faith in our darkest hours.
For the devil is so subtle, tempting us, using enemy or friend,
God allows him to roam, Jesus is our hope on Him can we depend.

Our challenge is when we have been hurt, and we know we should forgive,
The Lord said, "Vengeance is mine, I will repay," and in this truth we live.
Our challenge is to be like Jesus, and reflecting His love,
Back to our Father God, and everyone, as He does from above.

Our challenge also is to those we hold, in our hearts so dear,
Those who have stood with us, with each passing year.
Our challenge is to hold them, close to our Lord in prayer,
And our final challenge, with our Lord in heaven, we will all be there.

Life in Full.

Chosen by God, we have differing gifts, it is His plan,
To find our own gift, God has given discernment to man.
God is impartial, also to woman has given insight,
For He loves both dearly, and are precious in His sight.

Sometimes the circumstance of life, may seem unfair,
And we have a heavy burden, and no one seems to care,
All we need is a listening ear, to cast away our fear,
This is the time to speak with Jesus, as He is always near.

As ambassadors for Christ, may we be that listening ear,
May we be more receptive, as perfect love casts out all fear.
It is our love for others, our discipleship to Christ is known,
And our salvation is secure, for this did Christ atone.

Some preach God's word, for teaching is their gift,
Some have the gift of exhortation, for the church to uplift.
God gives encouragement to His gifts, whether large or small,
But the greatest gift He gave was Jesus, who gave for us His all.

Welcome are we, to come boldly to the throne of grace,
Sufficient is this in all the trials we have to face.
No longer are we alone, for the Spirit has come within us to dwell,
To bring us to remembrance, of all the things, Jesus, He did tell.

Prisoners for Christ, He holds the key from His home above,
There are no bars to this prison, it is enclosed by His love.
This prison is our haven, to escape we have no need,
Saved to eternity, and from God's wrath indeed.

Jesus is coming again, we read from God's word,
To the faithful believer, the greatest joy ever heard.
Today is the day of salvation, so lost sinner beware,
If Jesus came today, we pray we will meet you with Him there.

Listening for God

I listened for God and His voice I heard,
He said, "Sinner come unto me,
Not by works of your own but by Grace are you saved,
And your sins I have nailed on the tree.
For Jesus my Son for one purpose He came
To bring salvation endless and free.
He stood in your place for the judgment to come,
To reconcile you back to Me."

Like Adam by his fall I was born in sin without hope,
Until I found Jesus to Him was my plea;
My wretched soul is all that I have and I give back,
For your love is so boundless and free.

When His work here was done to His heavenly home He returned,
And His Spirit He sent here to be.
When the road here gets rough and your burden too strong,
Jesus said, "Cast your yoke upon me,"

Too long had I traveled life's road here alone,
How much longer alone must I be.
"Trust the Bible," said God, "and by faith its promise receive,
One God, Father, Son, Holy Spirit we three,"

Man has failed in his quest to find God on his own,
And his failure so plain to see,
For God's love is his bond His promise is sure,
And nothing can separate God's love from me.

Not an Easy Road

Lord God we know it's not an easy road,
To walk with Christ as King.
We know you will help us carry our load,
When with faith in you your praise we sing.

Lord God we find a void in our heart,
When without Christ we try to walk.
We know you will help us make a new start.
When we confess our sin, in our talk.

Lord God we do in Christ rejoice,
And in humbleness we cry,
We sing thy praise with upturned voice
When our trials you help us by.

Lord God we know that in Christ now,
From sin we have been set free;
Lord God in meekness our heads we bow,
As we find release in Thee.

Lord God I know within my heart,
I have failed you time and again.
But I know in your love I have a part,
And one day with Christ I'll reign

One Thing, Know

One thing may we desire, and that to earnestly seek,
To dwell in God's house forever, and of His glory speak.
In times of trouble, He will for us, in His pavilion hide,
Set us upon a rock, from our enemies, when we with Him abide.

To everything there is a purpose, as well there is a season,
A time to weep, to mourn, to everything there is a reason.
It is good for man, to eat and drink, and by his labour he may,
For what God does is forever, and no one can add, or take away.

The rich young ruler was sad, grieved and taken aback.
Jesus said, "Your heart is with your treasure, and one thing you lack.
Go sell what you have, give to the poor, let heaven be your treasure,
Take up the cross, and follow me, and you will find great pleasure."

One thing is needful, and Mary has chosen that good part,
Martha was too busy, with her chores, to listen to her heart.
Martha's priorities were on serving, and thought Jesus would agree,
He said, "One thing is needful, which Mary chose, to take away is not to be."

The Jews would not believe, it was Jesus who gave back the man his sight,
Asking his parents, is this your son who was blind, they said, "Yes that's right."
"We know not how or who opened his eyes, ask him who set him free,"
He said, "I know not whether sinner or not, I was once blind but now can see."

Saint Paul said, "This one thing, I do forget those things which are behind,
I press towards the prize, of God calling, with Christ Jesus in my mind.
Brethren, be followers of me, together with others who also walk,
Many are the enemies of the cross of Christ, of whom you have heard me talk."

This one thing know, A thousand years with the Lord is but one day,

His promise is sure, He would have none perish, so repent without delay.

His day will come as an thief in the night, so sinner do beware,

When He calls His own, to His heavenly home, my friends will you be there.

Our God of Creation

There is a story that is told of our God of old,
How He created a world, then a garden for man;
But man his soul to the devil sold,
And still hoped to fit in God's plan.

God in His displeasure banished the man,
From His garden so lovely and free.
To a life filled with burden for upsetting Gods plan,
God was heartbroken it was plain to see.

Man tried in vain God's favour to win,
With sacrifice he thought to please.
But God seeks obedience, and that from within,
From your own ways you must cease

If only man could have found in his heart to repent,
God might have taken a more lenient view.
But man for God his love was far spent,
And God did what he had to do.

But Gods love for man was never more sure,
And for proof He sent His dear Son.
His death on the cross for our sin He bore,
And the victory over death was won

At last man from his sin was saved,
By a God all loving and true.
In faith by grace man's path was paved,
And He did it for me and you.

Our Heavenly Rest

One day the sun and moon, will set no more,
When we are called home, to stand on that beautiful shore.
To look across the waters, and to see the glory land,
When God parts the waters, only then will we understand.

When we cross the river Jordan, to reach the promised land,
Our fear will be conquered, held by His loving hand.
On that day will be rejoicing, from the Angels and those gone before,
What a glorious day, to be with our Lord, and those forever more.

This world is not our home, we are just passing through,
Our old life to be discarded, when we receive the new.
We will hear the heavenly music, as with praise the Angels sing,
For Jesus our Lord and Saviour, from death has taken away the sting.

Jesus said, "Be not troubled, a place for you I have gone to prepare,
In my Father's house are many mansions, and there's a room for you there."
As we travel guided by His Spirit, may heaven be our goal,
Cleansed by His blood, saved by grace, we have been made whole.

God is still calling, His voice if we listen can still be heard.
May we respond to His voice, accepting the promise of His word.
Jesus did not come as a tyrant, condemning the world to sin,
He gave His life, paved the way, that in heaven we might enter in.

Today is the day of salvation, not always His voice will we hear,
If we submit our lives to Him, no longer we need to fear.
By faith is our hope, His word is truth and His promise is sure,
Patiently we wait, to be with the saved, with Him forevermore.

Our Hope in Asking

Have you ever been faced with an unenviable task?
Not knowing how to cope and no one to ask.
In times like this I know of a friend,
He will not forsake you He will stay to the end.

His name is Jesus, God's only begotten Son,
A willing Lord and Saviour, His work here is done;
It only takes a few moments in prayer,
And His blessing forever with you He will share.

Why struggle on alone, when help is close at hand,
The decision is yours to make, so just make the stand.
You will never regret, accepting His love,
For He watches over us from His home above.

One day we will meet Him, face to face,
All those who love Him are saved by his grace.
For the unbelieving it will not be the same,
When the book is open, He will not see your name.

Paid in Full

To the saved in Christ, the battle is over,
Jesus the sacrificial lamb He has won.
God sent His dear Son down to earth,
Now He's returned and His work here is done.

As His ambassadors we have the power to carry on His work,
Given by His Holy Spirit, the strength to face each task.
At times we are chastened, because of His love for us,
And when we feel the need of forgiveness, all we have to do is ask.

God knows our needs, and always wants what is good for us,
Lovingly waiting, for us to come to him in prayer.
At times our prayers may seem unanswered, maybe we ask amiss,
But we can be assured it's for our good, as He really does care.

God allows us to be tempted, but never more than we are able,
As He makes a way of escape, that we are able to bear.
But count it joy, for it tests our faith, and gives us patience,
Patience brings perfection, and if any lack wisdom, all it takes is a prayer.

Be angry and sin not, and put on the new man,
Grieve not the Holy Spirit, to one another be kind,
Let all bitterness, and evil speaking be put away,
And what a blessing of peace and contentment we will find.

If we say we have no sin, ourselves we do deceive,
But sin confessed, He is faithful and just and will forgive.
Jesus is the lamp unto our feet, and by his blood we are cleansed,
By His word and his Spirit, He teaches us how to live.

When the roll is called up yonder, and finally He calls us home,
We have a mansion, eternal in the heavens, made without hands.
When we appear before the judgment seat, and He opens up the book,
May God see the debt been fully paid, and for us Jesus stands.

Praise at all Times

Praise the Lord, when we feel the pain of stress,
Praise Him, for His goodness and righteousness.
Praise Him, always, and not as a last resort,
For this is true worship as we ought.

Praise the Lord, for the blessing He does give,
Praise Him for His word, teaching us how to live.
Praise Him, for Jesus our Lord, Saviour, and friend,
For His promise to stay with us, for eternity has no end.

Praise the Lord, when our burdens seem too hard to bear,
Praise Him, we can give them to Him, for He really does care.
Praise Him for nature, and the food that we eat,
Keeping us safe from evil, until in heaven we meet.

Praise the Lord, in temptation, a way out He has made,
Praise Him, for delivering us from the snare the devil has laid.
Praise Him, following the storm clouds, the sun does shine,
For the assurance of His love, is both yours and mine.

Praise the Lord, for our fellowship, of a believing friend,
Praise Him, that together on Him, we can depend.
Praise Him, when the road of uncertainty, comes our way,
For whatever befalls us, at the foot of the cross we can lay.

Praise the Lord, we can come boldly to the throne of grace,
Praise Him, when we have been hurt, He will help us to face.
Praise Him, that instead of retaliation, we can forgive,
For his Spirit teaches by grace, how in harmony we can live.

Praise the Lord, that with thanksgiving in awe we stand,
Praise Him, for our hope, to reach the promised land.
Praise Him for Jesus, for when He comes again,
For no more tears or sorrows, when with Him forever to reign.

Pray Without Ceasing

Unanswered prayer, is not always, "No" but just delay,
God may have something better, to show to us the way.
Don't be discouraged, for His timing is sure,
Pray without ceasing, and He will open the door.

Sometimes unanswered prayer, is because we ask amiss,
His word will give us the answer, at times like this.
We may feel He is not listening, but time is at His will,
Then gently He chastens, until His ways we fulfill.

Prayer is not telling God our wants, but asking our need,
He knows before we ask, we do not have plead.
A prayer asked in faith, we can be sure is heard,
For this is his promise, we read in his word.

Prayer is speaking to God, and through grace we are taught,
He is a willing listener, to our heart, mind, and thought.
His will is for us to ask, and by our faith He will give,
Our greatest prayer will be answered, when forever with Him we will live.

We pray for the church, when our Lord comes His bride to be,
For the church is God's children, which includes you and me;
For we are His temple, where His Holy Spirit does dwell,
As a comforter, sent from the Father, so the Bible does tell.

In prayer we find assurance, of God's love, and care,
In faith is our confidence, to know He is there;
With Jesus as our advocate, for us He will atone,
Then heaven will be our home, never more to be alone.

Put on the New Man

Off with the old man and on with the new,
And the fruits of the Spirit, in our hearts renew.
By God's word as we read, we are shown the way,
Born again, by his Spirit, who in our hearts comes to stay.

Our hearts may be willing, but the flesh is weak,
Trying to make it on our own, when His strength we ought to seek.
God does not force us, that's just not His way,
He gently chastises with love, until we obey.

He soothes away the pain when hurt by someone,
Teaching us how to forgive and forget, just as He has done.
He sent his Son Jesus, for our sins to forgive,
To die on that cruel cross, that we might forever with Him live.

He knows our weaknesses, always ready with a helping hand,
He promised to never leave or forsake us, and by us to stand.
As we face each new day, whatever it may bring,
May we give him the glory, when his praises we sing.

There is a day coming, when we shall meet him face to face,
What a blessing to be numbered, with those saved by grace.
Then when we reach heaven, and safe in the glory land.
But until we reach the journey's end, will we fully understand.

But until that day comes, for His guidance we must ask,
Praying for direction to complete, His every task.
He lovingly waits for us to ask, and He supplies our every need,
To bring lost souls into the fold, and on His word feed.

We did not choose Him, He made us His choice,
There is still hope for the lost, who will listen to His voice.
Our hope is in Jesus, all who have faith God will cherish,
But all who reject Him, according to his word sadly will perish.

Although this may seem harsh, Gods word is true,
We can neither add nor take away, just to suit me or you.
There are those who may mock, but God is always the same,
For Jesus is Lord and Saviour, for this is why he came.

Release From the Burden of Sin

Are you over laden with the burden of sin,
Have you heard the Saviour call?
For all our burdens He holds the key,
And He is willing to carry them all.

For the burden of sin, the price has been paid,
Christ suffered and died the price paid in full.
At the foot of the cross our sins have been laid,
Our efforts God chose to annul.

It is by grace we are saved, no merit of our own,
There is no way we could set ourselves free.
We are saved by Gods grace and forgiveness alone,
The shame of the cross alone He bore, for you and me.

God's grace and mercy, His unconditional love,
By His word it is plain to see,
He sent His dear Son from heaven above,
Put your trust in Him His only plea.

We are created in his image, what more could we ask,
We need to be born again, and filled with his love.
Not of our works, but by believing our only task,
Then one day we will meet Him in His home above.

Can we afford not to accept and trust Him,
As we travel through the world's evil powers.
For He has promised He will never leave us,
As with his bountiful blessing He showers.

Saviour and King

There is above all others a name,
It's Jesus who down to earth He came.
He came with a purpose to fulfill,
Obedient to the end, to His Father's will.

Born to the virgin Mary, in a lowly cattle stall,
His purpose for the lost sinners to save them all.
Sent by His Father down from heaven above,
To a lost world, to show His Father's love

Sinless was He, righteous, no need to repent,
Healing teaching and prayer, His time He spent.
When asked by his disciples, to teach them to pray,
He gave them a prayer pattern, and not just what to say.

For us to come to the Father, there is only one way,
It's through Jesus, not by works or what we say.
He gave his life a ransom, saved by His precious blood,
When we believe and trust him, His blessings on us will flood.

They brought to Him the sick, and healings He did perform,
And to all who put their trust in Him, He calms the raging storm.
No more to face the world alone, His promise is foretold,
By the Holy men inspired by God, in the times of old.

Ascending to His Fathers throne, His promise to return again,
Calling those of his kingdom, forever more with Him to reign.
And on that judgment day, God's wrath we will not have to face,
For Jesus our Lord and Saviour, He will stand there in our place.

For God who loves us so, how can we now reject?
Who gave us his Word and Spirit, teaching us to be perfect.
By faith His grace will save us, not by works, or merit embrace,
Salvation is freely given, "Praise Him" singing, saved by grace.

Seeking the Kingdom of God.

If the kingdom of God, we earnestly first seek,
As we read God's word, we hear the Holy Spirit speak.
The assurance of God's love, and presence we receive,
We find this promise in His word, to all who believe.

The kingdom of God, in our hearts we find within,
To be born of the Spirit, and cleansed from all sin.
Clothed in His righteousness, may our lights so shine,
Giving Him the glory, as we sing Jesus is mine.

The kingdom of God, is not in word but in power,
Protected by God's armour, which Satan cannot devour.
Saved by grace through faith, our salvation is sure,
When we meet Jesus in the Promised Land, to live evermore.

We have received a kingdom, but not of this world,
May we by grace serve God, with reverence and Godly fear.
No man is saved by his own works, but by grace through faith,
His grace is sufficient, not by merit, for He loves us so dear.

Christ's triumphant kingdom, is founded on love,
Welcome to all who believe, is echoed from above.
Condemnation is not from Christ, to all who believe,
It comes from rejection, to those who will not receive.

The kingdom of God is eternal, His blessing is sure,
The promise never to forsake us, to be with us evermore.
The world's pleasures like grass, will wither away,
But the joy when Jesus returns, will be a glorious day.

Nothing can overcome this kingdom, its built like a strong tower,
From the inside we are safe, from Satan s tempting power.
We could never afford to enter but by Gods grace,
Encircled by His love, when the judgment we face.

Seven R's + One

Relax. And take time when God's word we read,
For the Spirit speaks to us, when on His word we feed.
For prophecy came not in the old time by the will of man,
But the Holy men of God spoke, inspired by His plan.

Recall. As we read God's word, and hear the Spirit's voice,
To whom and what purpose is it wrote, and do we have a choice.
How does it apply to me, do I accept His will or reject?
It is inspired by God that the man of God may be made perfect.

Rehearse. When something that speaks to you in the word you find,
For by faith we receive, nothing else gives us this peace of mind.
His grace is sufficient, in whatever circumstance or place,
When we accept Jesus as Lord, no more trials alone do we face.

Retain. As we read Gods word, and we hear the Spirit speak,
For our life He has a purpose, and He blesses all who His will do seek.
His promise is sure; He is the good shepherd who gives all for His sheep
Sheltering us in the storms of life, safe in His fold to keep.

Rejoice. For the word tells us, our hope in Jesus is sure,
He has conquered death, for the saved life goes on forever more.
Saved by grace through faith, no more are we under the law,
Our sins are forgiven, may we sing His praises as never before.

Realign. As we read the word, may we in our hearts instill,
No more of works, but His grace, and respond in love to His will.
That when we fail to please Him, He chastens us in love,
Preparing us for His glory, to meet Him in His home above.

Release. As we read the word, we see we are meant to share,
God's love for us with others and their burdens help to bear.
Our life is but a channel, to pass on the Gospel story,
When Jesus comes to meet His bride, we all will share in His glory.

Reconciliation. Saved by grace through faith, assurance we find,
When Jesus Christ is our Lord and Saviour, we have this peace of mind.
That nothing can separate us from His love, this promise is in His word,
For His love is without merit, the greatest story ever heard

Sharing our Faith

Lord God it's good to share our faith,
And your love with others too.
How that Jesus sacrificed his life for us,
To bring us life anew.

Sometimes we feel so full of grace,
Sometimes we feel so down;
God is always on His throne to give,
And help us win our crown.

At times when in our darkest hours.
We see His light shine from above,
We only have to seek his face,
And He responds in love.

His Spirit in us has come to dwell,
With His power and His might,
When we accept Him as our redeeming Lord,
He brings darkness into light.

His Spirit in us we oft have quenched,
When our own paths we tread.
His word encourages us back to the fold,
When by His Spirit we are lead,

For God He so loved His church,
That His own Son He gave;
By His own blood we are redeemed
He did it for us to save.

Spiritually Alive

We need the Spirit of God within, or we are spiritually dead,
When we neglect to read God's word, we are not being spiritually fed.
There is a great day coming, when the saints can all rejoice,
When in heaven the saints and angels, will be singing with one voice.

May we be ever watchful, ready, and waiting for the dawning,
Of that great day when Jesus comes, for it will be without warning.
Gathering his wheat into his garner, and for the tares to burn,
And the judgement, to all who do not believe in his return.

There's none will ever perish, who on Jesus they trust and believe,
God does not condemn, they are condemned if Jesus they do not receive.
God so loves the world, His call goes out to all who will hear,
He watches over the faithful, as His presence is ever near.

There is only one way to the Father, through Jesus His only Son,
A once for all sacrifice, the victory over death He has won.
Bringing to us eternal life, no more can Satan win,
His work here done, His precious blood cleansed us from our sin.

In trials we may try to face alone, and in the darkness stumble,
Then like the prodigal son, missing home, keeps us humble.
No scolding voice when we return, but a welcoming hand,
His unmerited grace and mercy, bringing us to the glory land.

We may carry heavy burdens, beyond what we can bear,
We need to trust in Jesus, casting on Him our every care.
He willingly awaits to share our load, if we humble ourselves in prayer,
We never need to face alone, for He is always there,

Filled with his Holy Spirit, no more a servant but a son,

As His ambassadors, following on in the works he has done.

Herein is love made perfect, boldness in the judgment may we be,

Because as He is in this world, so are we.

Spiritually Filled

To be filled with the Spirit, we are cleansed by Jesus blood,
He's God's given gift, sent from above, with blessings to us flood.
He was sent by the Father, as a comforter and a friend,
To guide us in the footsteps of Jesus, until our journeys end.

We may hear many voices, for the truth there is one way to be sure,
God's word and His Spirit never contradict, the same forever more.
To beguile us, Satan is so deceitful, will try every trick in the book,
To every temptation God's given a way of escape, when to His word we look.

When guided by the Spirit, His good fruits to mind we bring,
Exhorting us into actions, showing love to others in everything.
A fountain cannot bring forth water, both bitter and sweet,
May our good works, please God, and bring blessings to all we meet.

May the light of Jesus reflect from us, to all along the way,
Blotting out the darkness of evil, as the light turns night to day.
May our lights so shine before men, and to God the glory bring,
Then in fellowship together, we can all praise God as we sing.

May our testimony be of good works, and our gospel not hide,
Clothed in the righteousness of Jesus, and His Spirit close beside.
May our faith never falter, and may our hope be our reward,
Then when the roll is called up yonder, we may meet with our Lord.

No one comes to Jesus, whom the Father does not call,
Jesus is the Way, the Truth, and the Life, no other way at all.
If we to the Father would come, and have not already done,
Today is the day of salvation, repent and trust in God's only Son.

We may reject the call, losing eternal life, it is our choice,
One day the call will end, may we take heed when we hear his voice.
If death overtakes us, or Jesus returns, to choose will be too late,
For Jesus will have the power to judge, and close the heavenly gate.

Suffering Endured

Sometimes it is hard when we see loved ones enduring pain,
And our prayers seem left unanswered, and almost seem in vain.
But God has not forgotten, He may have a purpose for us to know,
That in our suffering, our unfeigned faith, to a lost world we do show.

God does not withhold pain from us, and in Christ we feel no ill,
He allows pain, but does not send, for this is not His will;
Pain is not God's punishment, for He chastens us in love,
His Son, in agony died on the cross, as He looked down from above.

The evil one is always lurking and tries hard, when we a Godly life do live,
Luring our thoughts and hearts to him, and to him our ways would give.
He was defeated at the cross, although God still allows him to roam,
His power has gone, if we keep our sight on Jesus and our heavenly home.

God has set us apart, if we abide in Him, and in our hearts He will instill,
The Holy Spirit to indwell, lovingly teaching us to do his Holy will.
We are not driven, we are drawn, by grace as we begin to understand,
He only wants what is best for us, leading us by his loving hand.

He never will forsake us, His grace and mercy ever sure,
He has a place reserved for us, one day to be with Him for evermore.
We will have no more sorrow, or pain, Oh what heavenly bliss,
For we have the promise in his word, that in Jesus we are His.

He stands by us in our suffering, we look to Him in our need,
He never will reject us, while in faith on his word we do feed.
When we build on that solid foundation, with Jesus the corner stone,
And no earthly power can harm us, while God is on the throne.

God's word the Bible, the most precious book we will ever read,
When guided by His Spirit, He will supply all we will ever need.
If we do not feel His presence, it's us, not Him that has moved away,
For the debt for sin we owed, God's Son Jesus gave His life to pay.

Sustaining Grace

God's grace is sufficient and all that we need.
It's consistent and free we do not have to plead.
There is endless supply in His word when we read,
And we will never be wanting, by grace we are freed.

By grace we are freed from the burden of sin,
By grace we are indwelt by the Spirit within.
Sent from above to help us overcome and win,
When He calls us home, to be known as kin.

Grace keeps us going for it comes with power
When tempted to give up in our darkest hour.
Grace is like the sunshine that opens every flower,
And the more we trust the more He will shower.

Grace controls our thoughts and the way that we think,
Grace holds us up if we feel we are going to sink.
Grace is like a fountain that never runs dry,
And if we trust gets stronger as each day passes by.

We are saved by grace, and faith in Jesus' blood,
Bringing joy to our hearts like an overwhelming flood.
Sometimes we fail Him, but He understands,
If we confess our faults, forgives with outstretched hands.

So if we ever feel life is too hard to bear,
Look heavenward to Jesus for He is always there.
He will never forsake us, His promise is true,
For He is preparing an mansion just for me and you

The Author of Life.

God is the author of life, He has written the book,
Although He speaks of it often, the end we have to wait to look.
It's a true story; He knows every character and their need,
It's written for us to enjoy, if only we will take heed.

Like a master chess player, our every move has God planned,
Gently guiding us from all evil, by His loving hand;
Old Satan is always lurking, hoping to lead us astray,
But to escape from temptation, God has shown us the way.

God is the author of love, in His book makes it clear,
We can resist the temptation of evil, if by Him we stay near.
As the author of life, He knows every step that we take,
And draws us towards Him, for His own name's sake.

As the author He has written, teaching us to forgive,
In harmony and fellowship, with others to live;
He so loved the world, though tainted by sin,
That He opened the life gate, that all might come in.

As the author of the story, it's written to His will,
Lovingly written, teaching obedience in our hearts to instill.
He is never impatient, never tires, for time belongs to Him,
He knows how the story ends; it's not revealed, and not a whim.

In the book we know the ending, but are not told when,
If He decides to end it early, it will be the final Amen;
To be on the final page, and to reach the glory land,
Believe and trust in Jesus, as He beckons with an open hand.

The Cords of Love

On Calvary's Cross, it was our sin that put Him there,
No stronger cord could have held Him, but the cord of love.
He was led like a lamb to the slaughter, and he did bear,
The suffering and shame, at his Father's will from above.

Tempted by Satan, who laid the world at Jesus feet,
Rejecting the temptation, for Jesus sinless was He.
It was on the cross, His purpose for Satan to defeat,
Submit to God, resist the devil, and from you he will flee.

It was on the cross; Jesus abolished the old ceremonial law,
A once for all sacrifice, no need for the blood of animals as before.
By His spirit, He has placed a new law, within our heart,
A law of love, that to others we may His love impart.

When finally we face the judgment, may we find,
The charge dropped, the dark storms of life left behind.
The longsuffering and loving kindness, in the word we are told,
Of a loving Saviour, calling us safely into the fold.

Even nature itself, teaches us of a God who is in control,
Who sent His Son, who gave His life to save our soul.
None other sacrifice, was acceptable, to Him for our sin,
Ascending to His Father's side, sent His Spirit to dwell within.

The clouds may cover, but the sun each day passes by,
The word says one day, Jesus will return down from the sky.
Coming for His church, for us, His Bride to be,
Our hope fulfilled, when the glory of His kingdom, we will see.

When this great event happens, for our loved ones is our prayer,
They have put their trust in Jesus, safe in His loving care.
Jesus did not come to condemn, and our own judges may we be,
When the roll is called up yonder, we will all our Saviour see.

The Fathers Love for Us.

Oh what joy to follow in Jesus' footsteps,
As through this barren land we go.
What a privilege to be called by Him,
Who gave His life, because He loves us so.

None other ever cared for us so much,
Than the Father who sent His only Son.
Despised, rejected, took upon Himself our sin,
Death no longer holds us, for eternal life He has won.

The price for sin, to pay we could not afford,
The sacrifice He made, just so He could forgive.
Opening the door to His heavenly home,
So as one day with Him we will forever live.

In Jesus God has to us revealed Himself,
Showing His nature, teaching us what He wants us to be.
Loving one another, in gentleness towards those in need,
In Jesus name from their burdens to be set free.

The Word became flesh, and came among us to dwell,
Ascending to His Father's side, His Spirit He did send.
A Guide and Comforter, to all who believe,
Leading to Eternal life, which will never end.

Jesus did not come to condemn the world,
But to save, and salvation is free to all who will.
Accept the Father's grace, for there is no other way,
But through Jesus, and may our hearts His Spirit fill.

His promise to never leave or forsake us,
In our trials, through him we can feel secure.
No matter how steep to climb is the mountain of life,
He is only a prayer away, we can rely on Him for sure.

The Fountain of Love

Will you come and drink at the fountain?
Overflowing with love and care.
Will you drink of that life giving water?
Then in heaven we will all meet there.

Have you an unquenchable thirst,
That nothing alone seems to cure?
Then come to the fountain overflowing with love,
And your thirst will be quenched evermore.

Just a drink from that life giving fountain,
Will help guide you along life's way.
And the trials you face will seem smaller,
And your prayers will be heard when you pray.

So friend don't carry your burdens alone,
When help is only a prayer away.
Come drink of that overflowing fountain of love,
Quench your thirst now don't delay.

This overflowing fountain of love,
Is Jesus God's only begotten Son.
Come drink of that life giving water,
You'll find the battle of life has been won.

Just a drink of this water, brings life in full,
For a purpose God sent His dear Son.
He died on the cross for the pardon of sin,
Rose again now His work here is done.

Come to the fountain, drink, thirst no more,
His promise He is coming again.
Will you be there when we meet at the fountain,
When in eternity with Him we will reign.

The Law our Schoolmaster

The law was our schoolmaster, leading us to Christ,
It taught us to fear, as at God's mercy we stand.
Through the wilderness, Moses led the children of Israel forty years,
But it was only from the distance he saw the Promised Land.

Way before Moses, Noah heard and hearkened to God's voice,
Build a big boat, for this dry land I am going to flood.
For some it must have seemed foolish, as of rain they had never heard,
The law led us to the cross, and we are saved by Christ's precious blood.

God chose Abraham, as the father of an innumerable nation,
Which may have seemed strange, as his wife was without child.
But God's word is sure, unchangeable; with Him nothing is impossible,
Like the virgin birth which God gave Mary, of a child so meek and mild.

Through the sin of disobedience, from the garden was Adam banned,
Before the law was there was no penalty, no sacrifice for sin.
God gave Moses the Ten Commandments, to show the people His will,
And as a Saviour He sent Jesus, and His Holy Spirit to dwell within.

Dare to be a Daniel, and stand true to God's Holy word,
God poured blessings upon him, in his greatest hour of need.
Rather than bow to false idols, he and his friends faced death,
Jesus said, He would never leave, or forsake us, a blessing indeed.

Job faced trial upon trial, but he endured never giving in,
God allowed Satan to tempt and torment, but his life to leave.
His friends were no comfort, his wife told him to curse God and die,
Eternal life is our goal, when Jesus our Lord and Saviour we receive.

Jacob worked seven years for Rachel, but was given Leah instead,
He worked another seven years, and God gave him his reward.
Although undeserved, our reward is without works but of grace,
We can put our trust in God, with Jesus as Saviour and Lord.

The Lord's Prayer

His disciples asked Jesus, "Teach us how to pray."
He gave them a pattern for prayer, not just what to say.
"Our Father in heaven" is a relationship for us to know,
"Our" showing an unselfish spirit, and "Father" our reverence to show.

"Hallowed be thy name" a reverent spirit, the giving of our will,
To Worship His Deity, a subject relationship to fulfill.
"Thy Kingdom come" acknowledging His sovereignty patiently await,
Accepting His grace and mercy, lifting us from a lowly state.

"Thy Will be done" a submissive spirit, willingly upholding,
The Father's will as we see through Jesus His love unfolding.
"Give us this day our daily bread" shows on Him we do depend,
But man cannot live by bread alone, and His Spirit He did send.

"Forgive us our debts" a penitent spirit, with a thankful heart,
Teaching us to forgive others, that we may from sin depart.
"Lead us not into temptation" a humble spirit as we pray,
Keeping us from all evil, and close to Jesus, for He is the only way.

"Thine is the kingdom" a confident spirit, in Him do we trust,
Not trusting in our own works, pride, jealously and lust.
"And the power" a triumphant spirit, our comforter and shield,
And as to Him we bow our heads in prayer, to Him our hearts yield.

"And the glory" an exultant spirit, in joyful heartfelt praise,
As we Worship and adore Him, in song our voices to Him raise.
What else can we give our "Father" who loves us and so true,
He only wants what's best for us, and He's with us in everything we do.

"Forever and forever" is eternal, a beginning but no end,
We have this promise in His word, on which we can depend.
Our Father knows before we ask, what we need and when,
Lovingly provides for us, when we feed on his word, Amen.

The Reason Why He Came

I tried so hard to please my God,
But my efforts were all in vain.
I thought that all I did was good,
But ere it was but feign.

I traveled a very lonely road,
Contentment and peace I could not find.
The guilt of sin it was my load,
With shame was filled my mind.

In prayer I pleaded with my God,
I know your law so well.
"What more can I do, my God?" I said,
Still in my heart the guilt and shame did dwell.

One day I heard the voice of God,
I said, "I am listening, Oh my Lord,"
He said, "The price of sin it is so great,
And a price you cannot afford."

My God, He said, "You've tried too hard,
For the battle is mine and won.
There is no power on earth so great as that,
Of my beloved Son."

"He came as man on earth to dwell,
To pay the price of sin.
To reveal my love to woman and man,
And for their hearts to win."

They nailed His body to the tree,
The end of Him they thought.
He sacrificed Himself for us,
And Eternal life has brought.

So sinner like me who bore the guilt,
Of loneliness sin and shame
Let Jesus be your Saviour, and Lord,
For that is why He came.

The Saviour's Call

We have a Saviour, and Redeemer indeed,
We only have to ask, we don't have to plead.
Believe, in his promise, He will always be there,
He always hears us, when we come to Him in prayer.

No more this dark world, do alone we have to face,
Believe in His promise, and come boldly to the throne of grace.
The debt for our sin, paid in full, by Jesus precious blood,
By His grace and mercy, showers of blessings upon us He will flood.

Our love towards each other, He teaches to give and forgive,
The Bible is a book of instruction, showing us how to live.
We may feel we are unworthy, but God is satisfied,
For it was within His will, Jesus was crucified and died.

The grave could not hold Him, victory over death He won,
God had worked His purpose out, a new life for us He had begun.
Jesus asked the Father, and his Holy Spirit He did send,
Who helps us overcome our trials, on Him we can depend.

When walking in the Saviours footsteps, no more we walk alone,
A once for all sacrifice for us, to the Father He did atone.
When guided by his Spirit, His fruits by our actions we show,
Our love towards each other, that the lost may come to know.

Protected by our faith, nothing can separate us from God's love,
Sheltered in His loving arms, watching us from heaven above.
There is no condemnation, who in Jesus take their stand,
And through temptations and trials, leads us by a loving hand.

To all who for Jesus have not yet made the choice,
He is calling today, sinner come home, is His welcoming voice.
He is coming to judge, the calling over, we know not the day,
Don't leave it too late; let Him into your heart to stay.

The Storms of Life

Sometimes in the storms of life,
There is a purpose to be found.
To help us through our trials and strife,
As we travel heavenward bound.

Although in life for blessings we look,
It is by the storms we outwardly grow.
If life was like the smell of flowers or a gentle brook,
The hurts of others we would never understand or know.

It is in the storms of life we are made fully aware,
Of the role God wants us to be part.
By His guiding hand and our hearts full of care,
Our merciful God will to us His blessing impart.

God encourages us as each day with its trials bring,
To walk close to Him, in His ways to cling.
The world with its pleasures looks only to find,
They are only short lived with no peace of mind.

As we travel along heavens road we must face,
All the worldly trials, but God gives us His grace.
With our heart aches and sorrows He understands,
And nothing can harm us when we are safe in His hands.

One day at His bidding we will meet at His throne,
And the trials of this world will no longer be known.
He will welcome us home to a mansion prepared,
And to be with Him forever for our life He has spared.

The Wonder of the Cross

It was down beside that wooden cross,
I thought at first it was my loss.
It looked to me to be the end,
But only did my Saviour bend.

The load that bent Him was my sin,
I could never repay what He felt within.
But he did it with no thought of gain,
Just so one day in heaven with Him we'll reign,

God so loved the world He gave His Son,
The victory over evil and death He has won.
We may suffer trials while in this land,
But now can trust in God while in His hand.

Trust in Jesus

Put your trust in Jesus He is Saviour and Lord,
He is also a friend, and One to be adored.
As each day passes by, let Him be your guide,
You will never fall, with Him by your side.

Put your trust in Jesus, learn not to fear,
He patiently awaits for you to draw near.
Step out of the darkness, and into the light,
Put your faith in him not in your sight.

We may try to evade Him, but there is nowhere to hide,
We cannot find peace whilst clinging to pride.
The moment we accept Him, His Spirit comes to dwell,
Within us forever, and our fears He will expel.

Without Him, there is a void, nothing can fill,
When we walk in darkness, by our own will.
Satan may encourage you, tomorrow will do,
He is lost forever, today salvation awaits for you.

Jesus is coming again, we are not told the hour,
We are told He is coming, with almighty power.
Coming to gather His church, this is why we state,
Today is the day of salvation, tomorrow maybe too late.

It only takes a moment of time, to ask Jesus to come in,
He is already paid the price, in full for our sin.
He hung on the cross, bound by cords of love,
Now eagerly awaits, to take you, to His home above,

His coming maybe tomorrow, next month, or whatever year.
With Jesus as Lord, we have nothing to fear.
He patiently awaits in his Father's home above,
To send showers of blessings, with an everlasting love.

We Are Not Alone

Don't try to face the world alone,
With its trouble and its care.
The Lord is always waiting,
And listening for your prayer.

Did you hear when Jesus called today?
Or did He call in vain.
Oh what sadness if we missed Him,
For He may never call again.

Have you ever wondered,
How the world became to be?
Did someone find a piece of wood,
And decide to make a tree?

If Jesus called again today,
What would your answer be?
I was once the prisoner of sin,
But now have been set free,

When Jesus to this world returns,
With his glory and His power.
Sinner will you be waiting,
For that most glorious hour?

On the tree they crucified our Lord,
"That's the end of him," they said.
It proves they did not understand or care,
Prophecies in the Bible they had read

They laid him in an empty tomb,
And stood on guard that night.
But Death and Hell cannot hold him,
Because Jesus Christ is light.

So sinner be not dismayed,
For God's love is very sure.
Answer him when we hear his call,
And he will stay with us evermore.

What Do We Really Believe?

When we read our Bibles, do we believe what we read?
For it contains guidance, strength, also warnings to take heed.
This book is the story, of what God has planned for man,
And the blessing we receive, when guided by His hand.

Do we take a verse out of context, as guidance for the day,
And rightly or wrongly, hold to it, come whatever may?
If we add to or take away, its meaning is lost no longer whole,
Inspired by God, written by man, as nourishment to our soul.

Faith is a God given gift, which He gave at great cost,
Belief is all or nothing or our faith will be lost.
God sent His Son, not to condemn, but to the world to save,
Saved by grace through faith, not by merit of how we behave.

Faith has no parts; it has to be whole and complete,
Without faith we will stand alone, when at the judgment seat.
Faith is trusting Gods promise, taking Him at His word,
For He is a God of justice, as from the Scriptures we have heard.

If the devil can get control of half, he has all to gain.
But if God only has half, He has none at all to detain.
For it was through unbelief, not faith, our Lord was crucified,
It was for our sin, He hung upon that cruel cross and died.

Sin and death He conquered, arose again on the third day,
By our faith in Him, has brought reconciliation, there is no other way.
Clothed in his righteousness, released from the burden of sin,
Has opened wide the gates of heaven, that we can enter in.

As we read our Bibles, maybe, not all we understand,
But to believe is faith, leading us to the Promised Land.
It teaches us God's will, we walk by faith not sight,
And in the darkest hours, we stumble not, for Jesus is the light.

Why Forsaken?

"My God, My God, why have you forsaken me,"
Dying alone upon the cross, this was Jesus plea.
Banished from the presence of God, it was for our sin,
God turned away, He could not watch, the agony He felt within.

Jesus was as always, obedient to his Father's will,
Said, "If this cup will not pass from me, let me drink my fill."
The crowds shouted, "He saved others, now let himself to save."
If only they understood, this way they would not behave.

He did it to bring salvation, in the judgment taken our place,
When God makes that final call, we will not have God's wrath to face.
God is calling, hearken to his voice, there is no other way,
Do not reject Him, or in the judgments, for your sins you will pay.

In salvation God has set us apart, for His use our lives must sanctify,
He does not force, this is His will, He doesn't teach the birds to fly.
Like a sculptor He fashions us, until his requirements we meet,
God is patient; it may take a while, and starts at the mercy seat.

When we surrender our lives to him, from us He works within,
We are His hands, His feet, His eyes, cleansing us from sin.
We cannot please God, until all our self will we set aside,
Then one day in heaven, we will meet in his mansion to abide.

Will there be any stars in our crown, when we are called to give account,
For the things we should or should not, for it is the deed not the amount.
God hates the sin, but loves the sinner; all He asks is for us to repent,
Gods plan fulfilled in Jesus, for this reason He was sent.

God sent his Son to die for us, have you let Him die in vain,

Accept his Grace and Mercy, for your salvation to obtain.

His love extends to all, and none should perish not one,

Jesus death upon the cross was not in vain, His Fathers will is done.

Wisdom the Preacher

Vanity of vanities, were the words of the preacher,
What profits a man, for his labour for life is his teacher.
One generation passes, another comes, but the earth will remain,
But wisdom is fruitful, to all who labour to obtain.

To fear the Lord is wisdom, but many fail to understand,
To stay from evil is the beginning of knowledge, for God's plan.
He created man for His own glory, giving him freedom of choice,
Eating of the tree, man knew he was wrong, and hid on hearing Gods voice.

Adam blamed Eve, who said she was enticed by the serpent,
God banned them from the garden, not allowing them to repent.
For his disobedience, Adam to eat now had to till the ground,
By the sweat of his face, in sorrow, no longer peace to be found.

We see God's plan unfolding, from the Bible as we read the pages,
How He spoke through His prophets, sending warnings down the ages.
Ezekiel in his vision the dry bones without life in the valley he saw,
Showing the lowly state of God's people, but one day he would again restore.

We read in Isaiah, his prediction of the coming child to be born,
Wonderful, Counselor, Prince of peace, His name, a new day would dawn.
Gods promise of Christ's kingdom and His Holy Spirit within us to dwell,
Restoring His people again into His fold, in His word it does tell.

We have an inheritance, which was given to our forefathers long ago,
Of God's love for His creation, man inspired by God, wrote for all to know.
Bringing unto us salvation, through His Son the Prince of peace,
Labouring on together, proclaiming His Gospel, may His church increase.

As we sow the seeds of kindness, we reap the harvest of love,
And in the raging storms we face, our strength comes from above.
Through trials, temptations, burdens, whatever may be our task,
He sent His Spirit to help and comfort us, and we only have to ask.

Yesterday's Gone

Yesterday has gone, and the things we did can never change,
We cannot go back if we wanted to in order to rearrange.
Today is a new day, which brings new things for us to face,
And tomorrow does not exist, only by God's grace.

The things we did yesterday, we lay at the foot of the cross,
For Jesus our Lord and Saviour, gave His life, suffering the loss.
Our sins have been paid for, ordained from the Father above,
It was not the nails that held Him; it was the cords of love.

If we could turn back the clock, to live our lives anew,
And lay aside the things that hinder, and find good works to do.
To walk in Jesus footsteps, as we journey along life's way,
Submitting our lives to our Father God, the devil will flee away.

The devil has no power over us; at the cross was his defeat,
But it does not stop him trying, using all kinds of deceit.
When safe in the arms of Jesus, sheltered within the fold,
We like sheep, He our Shepherd, showering blessing upon us untold.

If we only live for what we see, and death it is the end,
We are of men most miserable, denying the one whom God did send.
We have this promise, in verse sixteen of St John chapter three,
That all who believe in Jesus, will have eternal life, including you and me.

When Jesus left this world, returning to His Father's side,
He said, He is preparing a place in heaven, where one day we will abide.
Blessed are those that mourn, the meek, also the pure in heart,
And when persecuted, or reviled, His strength to us will He impart.

May our salt never lose its savour, or our candle it be hid,
May our witness be fruitful, humbled from the unfruitful things we did.
God does not rule by force, He chastens His elect in love,
And at His final call, may we be ready to meet Him in His home above.